BEREAVEMENT SUPPORT GROUPS
FOR CLINICIANS AND LAYMEN

Marina Oppenheimer, LMHC

TO G. WHO HAS PASSED,

BUT WHO WILL ALWAYS BE WITH ME

§

SUMMARY

Support Groups:
How Effective are They?

Session 1

Session 2

Session 3

Session 4

Session 5

Session 6

Session 7

Session 8

ACTIVITIES

Group rules

Activity 1

Activity 1a

Activity 2

Activity 3

Activity 4

Activity 5

Activity 6

Activity 7

SUPPORT GROUPS

HOW EFFECTIVE ARE THEY?

Several studies have shown group psychotherapy to be more effective than individual psychotherapy in a variety of settings. In this case however we will be talking of support groups, not therapy groups. The basic difference between a psychotherapy group and a support group is that while in the former members' interactions with others will be used as a basis for clinical interpretation and intervention, in the latter the goal is to provide members with assistance and information on the topic of bereavement.

In order to be effective groups, have to be homogeneous; in other words, members have to be of approximately the same age and cultural background. In the case of bereavement groups, it is well known that different cultures have different ways of coping with loss and as a result they will mourn differently.

Regarding the group leaders, if they happen to be laymen, they won't have any difficulties empathizing with group members because all of us have gone through the experience of loss and bereavement.

Although a support group is not a psychotherapy group, I will borrow from Irving Yalom some of his definitions of group therapy that also apply to support groups.

- **Universality**

The fact that all members will be sharing their experience of grief with others who are in the same situation will remove members' sense of isolation and feeling of being different.

- **Altruism**

The group is a perfect place for members to help each other and this is a curative factor in itself. Helping others allows members to forget themselves for a moment and focus on another member's distress.

- **Instillation of hope**

Members who are more advanced in their mourning process will become role models for those who are struggling with the initial stages of bereavement.

- **Imparting information**

This characteristic is extremely important for bereavement support groups since it provides members with much needed information on community resources, books, videos and other bereavement material.

- **Cohesiveness**

A cohesive group will provide its members with a sense of belonging.

- **Existential factors**

Members will learn that death is a part of life that needs to be accepted and integrated into the fabric of our existence.

- **Catharsis**

Catharsis is the emotional relief from a distressful situation. By exploring and verbalizing their grief members will feel relieved and less anguished.

- **Self-understanding**

This factor will allow members to understand how their current grief is not only the sum of all previous losses but also how it is related to their own passing.

Note: Due to the complexity present in the process of loss and bereavement, the group should not be composed by more than 8 members.

SESSION 1

Introductions

The facilitator introduces him/herself.

Members introduce themselves and explain what brought them to the group. They will be asked to write their first names on labels so that every member knows other members' names.

The facilitator asks members what in their opinion is a bereavement group. This will be a way for the facilitator to become aware of each member's goal for the group. After all members have expressed their understanding of bereavement groups, the facilitator provides his/her point of view.

Facilitator: *"A bereavement group is a safe place where people who have lost a loved one can express and explore their feelings. A group is also a place where we meet with other people who have gone through the same experience and where we learn about other ways to view the experience of loss. It is a well-known fact that there is neither a unique way to grieve nor a set time to heal. As a matter of fact, everybody will grieve at his/her own pace and in his/her own way. "*

Following the description of a bereavement group, the facilitator explains to members what the group rules are as well as the importance of attendance.

Group Rules: (At the end of the book.)

Once group rules have been explained and understood, the facilitator introduces Activity 1. (under Activities.)

After Activity 1 has been completed, the facilitator will verbalize his/her goals for the group.

1. To understand the process of loss and bereavement.

2. To increase participants' resilience to loss.

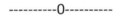

Once members have expressed their goals for the group and being made aware of the facilitator's goals, the following information will be provided.
The facilitator should encourage members to interrupt him/her to ask questions or make comments as often as needed.

THE IMPACT OF LOSS

I would like to start by saying that a loss is never overcome: the most we can expect is to adjust to our loss in order to function in our everyday life. But as Elizabeth Kubler-Ross pointed out, not only we will never overcome a loss but also, we will never be the same again. Accepting this truth is the first step in our journey towards our life without our loved one.

When it comes to loss, we are all born equal. There is a very beautiful Buddhist parable that tells the story of a woman who had lost her son. Desperate she went to see the Buddha to ask him to resuscitate her child. The Buddha looked at her and said: *"Go to every house in town and ask them if they use mustard to cook their meals. If you find one home that does not use mustard for cooking, bring me your son and I will resuscitate him."* The woman ran back to town and started knocking desperately on every door to ask if mustard was part of their menu. Unfortunately, she was unable to find one single home that did not have mustard in the kitchen. Even more desperate she went back to the Buddha and through her tears told him about her inability to find a kitchen with no mustard, and the Buddha said to her: **"In the same way as no kitchen is devoid of mustard, no life is devoid of the pain of loss."** The woman understood the teacher's words and went back home.

According to John Bowlby (*Attachment and Loss, 1969*) what we call loss is the rupture of an attachment and the deeper the attachment the deeper the loss. A loss is not only related to people but also to countries, health, youth, jobs or worldly possessions. As a result, immigration or losing a job are also significant losses. Furthermore, each new loss rekindles the pain of old losses in a sort of accumulative process. For instance, if during our childhood we lost one of our parents, every loss we will suffer later in life will make us relive the loss of that parent. So, we could say that every present loss is connected to every past loss. Consequently, when we reach old age, we will have suffered many losses. In a way this is a blessing in disguise since it helps us start processing our own separation from this world.

Grief is a very individual process. Depending on our personality and our life history, we will all grieve in our own particular way so much so that it is very difficult to describe in a general way how to approach loss and adjustment to loss. However, one trait that is common to all adjustment processes is that it takes time. While some people will be able to adjust faster to their new reality, others, especially if they are born with a tendency to melancholy, will have more difficulties enjoying life again.

There is a Chinese proverb that states that a **one thousand miles journey starts with the first step**. In the bereavement process the first step is the acceptance of what is. Consequently, depending on the personality traits of the bereaved two things can happen:

1. Being able to accept the reality of the loss and start the grieving process
2. Being unable to accept the reality of the loss and fall into a prolonged depression

Both reactions are clearly different psychological processes. While the acceptance of reality is conducive to start the grieving process, depression denies what is and transforms the bereaved into a victim of fate. This will postpone the mourning phase, the adjustment process, and the reorganization of life without the deceased.

Inevitably loss brings about disorganization in the life of family members. The sudden presence of death in our lives makes us more vulnerable and unable for a while to function properly. The most pervasive of all feelings after a loved one disappears from our life is a boundless absence that makes our future difficult to fathom. In the case of women who are dependent on their husbands financially his absence is compounded by the stress of economic survival. The Indian film *Water* depicts in detail what the life of widows becomes in India if they happen not to have any financial support. In Western countries women are in a much better situation than in Eastern countries. However, even for women who are well off the loss of a husband will leave a wife struggling for a new social identity.

When someone dies the first thing that the bereaved will experience is shock. The fact that we need to take care of the funeral and other tasks provides us with a much-needed time to regroup before facing our new reality and for the feeling of shock to subside. During the first months after the death of a loved one our mind will be obsessed with details of the passing. Sometimes feelings of guilt will arise if we were left with the impression that we could have done more to postpone the loss, or even feelings of anger at the deceased for abandoning us. At this stage sadness and depression will set in and it is not uncommon for the bereaved to see the deceased in familiar places. These hallucinations are not the result of mental illness but are generated by the deep sense of longing we feel for the departed.

As reality sinks in the bereaved will move on to the disorganization stage where life has to be rearranged without the presence of the deceased. This disorganization is characterized by a deep feeling of fear about the future, not only regarding the loneliness that awaits the bereaved but also often about finances and other life responsibilities. Reorganization occurs when people decide that they will try to find a meaning to the loss they have suffered. Once the loss is accepted, the bereaved will be able to regroup and incorporate the loss into their life. Although life will move on to new experiences, often the bereaved will find themselves constantly reliving their memories of the departed. This is especially true in old age.

Finally, although by and general we are able to adjust to our losses, the sadness of the loss will forever stay in our hearts. Eventually however, even for those of us who did not enjoy a good relationship with our departed, time will help us accept the fact that no relationship is free from conflict and that we can always focus on the happy times spent together. Furthermore, even if our loved one is not with us anymore, we still have the option of asking for forgiveness and to forgive past misunderstandings so as to go on with our lives in peace.

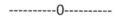

The facilitator will distribute copies of Activity 1a to group members and will ask them to identify what are their feelings at this stage of bereavement. This information will be processed until the end of the 1st session. If necessary, this activity will continue in the 2nd group session.

SESSION 2

A JOURNEY OF 1000 DAYS STARTS WITH THE FIRST STEP
(Chinese proverb)

Like I mentioned in our first session, we never overcome a loss, we just learn to live with it. A loss is not supposed to be forgotten and it can be said that we are the sum of all our losses. Furthermore, by the way we react to our losses we are shaping our own departure from this world. If we accept reality as it is, and we can face our challenges with courage we will also be able to depart this life with dignity.

The reason why losses are so devastating is because after every loss we change; we stop being who we were to become a different person. Without a doubt loss are our most difficult challenges in our life journey and some of us will need a long time to be able to resume a normal life after a significant loss. But as the title of this chapter points out, *a journey of one thousand miles starts with the first step.* As we undertake our mourning journey, we will need to remember that time is our more valuable ally.

The days and months that follow a significant loss are totally disorienting and characterized by numbness. Once the funeral services are over and our family and friends go back to their own lives, we are left with the void generated by the absence of our loved one. At this stage of our bereavement process there are no words that can even start to alleviate the pain we feel. I remember calling one of my friends in another state at a time when he had lost his son. I was so sad and confused that paradoxically the only thing I could say to him was: "Paul, I really don't know what to say to you." His answer was: "If you were here you could give me a hug."

The expression **grief work** was coined by Erich Lindemann in the 1940s. Lindemann studied the reactions of people who had lost a relative or a friend in the 1942 Cocoanut Grove fire in Boston. The Cocoanut Grove was a Boston nightclub during the post-Prohibition era of the 1930s and 1940s. On November 28, 1942 this club was the scene of a terrible fire that killed 492 people, injuring hundreds more. Many of the conclusions Lindemann reached during these interviews can be found in his book *Symptomatology and Management of Acute Grief (1944.)*

From Lindemann's point of view suffering generated by loss needs to be treated. He described the symptomatology of grief as composed by preoccupation with the deceased, somatic complaints (i.e. exhaustion, sighing, digestive complaints), feelings of guilt and even hostility (towards the bereaved, other relatives and friends, as well as the treating clinician.) Lindemann's grief work is based on emotionally detaching from the deceased and focusing on other rewarding relationships.

As already mentioned, time is our most significant partner in this difficult journey. Medications are also a valuable resource. A visit to a psychiatrist will help us understand how antidepressants and anti-anxiety agents can help us travel the difficult road ahead more peacefully. However, this is an individual choice because not everybody agrees with the benefits of psychotropic medications.

Undoubtedly at this stage of bereavement the most important resource we have will be our family and our friends. Nothing is more valuable than the affection and support provided by those who love us, not just by being there but also by sharing with us their own experiences of loss. Despite the lack of energy, we usually feel after a loss, the best thing we can do is make time to be with friends and family as often as they possibly can. This will not only distract us from our pain but will also provide us with the motivation to continue on our life journey.

Besides medication, family and friends, there are also community resources that are very valuable after we have suffered a loss. Most churches and temples offer bereavement support groups to the community. These groups are usually led by volunteers who have gone through the same experience and are eager to assist their fellow human beings. The internet is a good way to find a support group near our home or place of work. Being continually busy is the best way to spend the first months of bereavement so as not to have to face our sorrow until we are emotionally more resilient.

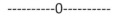

----------0----------

This session should be used to allow group members to tell their stories of loss. Feedback from other members and from the facilitator will help them start their mourning journey. Telling their personal stories will help members feel closer to each other and the group to become a cohesive unit.

The facilitator will distribute copies of Activity 2.

SESSION 3

You will not overcome the loss of a loved one. You will learn to live without your loved one.

You will heal and you will rebuild yourself around the loss you suffered.

You will be whole again, but you will never be the same. Nor should you be the same, nor would you want to be the same.

Elizabeth Kubler-Ross

      The path towards the reorganization of life after a significant loss is a long one. The more significant the loss, the longer and more difficult the path towards having a normal life again. Our life is shattered, and we are pervaded by disorientation, sadness, apathy, anxiety and fear. Often the feeling of disorientation will lead to a lack of meaning and confusion regarding our beliefs. Our life as we knew it suddenly evaporates and all we see are debris all around us like after a deadly storm. Deep down our hearts we all know that situations and feelings are not permanent. Throughout our lives we have all learned that *"this too shall pass."* However, human beings abhor change and we always have the tendency to go back to what we are familiar with. Unfortunately, life is nothing but change and like Elizabeth Kubler-Ross states losses are not to be forgotten but remembered.

The only way to assimilate a loss is to find a meaning to what happened to us. However, this is easier said than done especially in the case of the loss of a child. Moreover, what complicates matters further is the fact that since the meaning we are looking for is a meaning for us only, nobody can really help us in this complex task because nobody else has found the same meaning to loss. In his book *Man's Search for Meaning* (1946) Victor Frankl states that none of us can really avoid suffering, but what we can do is find a meaning to what has happened to us. Finding a meaning to loss will provide us with a new purpose and will help us move ahead.

Furthermore, our life task is none other than that: finding a meaning to all that happens to us so that we can learn from experience and become wiser and stronger. Let's not forget that finding a meaning does not mean finding a way to justify the death of a loved one. It's just a way to understand how that loss is related to our life journey. Furthermore, even if we are unable to understand the loss, the important thing is our decision to go within looking for our inner wisdom. Although life journey can be a very painful one, I am convinced that it will never bring us more pain that we can bear because otherwise humanity would end.

When we suffer a significant loss, it is possible to enjoy life again, but the loss will stay with us forever. One of my patients who lost a daughter a long time ago told me recently that she still remembers her every day. However, another patient said to me that her daughter has been gone for so many years that she does not remember what her favorite dish was anymore. It is not uncommon for people who have suffered the loss of a loved one to see a vision of their beloved in their home for several months after the passing. This is none other than a symptom of their severe depression and their difficulty in letting go. All these symptoms have to be accepted as part of the grieving process. Gradually they will disappear as we move towards the reorganization of our life.

Kubler-Ross spoke of five stages of grief in the case of relatives of people with terminal illness:

Denial: *"This can't be happening to me."*
Anger: *"Why is this happening* to me?"
Bargaining (before the loss happened**):** *"Please God make this not happen and I will* (fill the blank.)
Depression: *"I feel so sad that I don't have energy to do anything."*
Acceptance: *"I am in pain, but I have finally accepted what is happening in my life."*

It is important to understand that we all grieve in different ways and that not all of us will go through Kubler-Ross' stages. Or perhaps some of us will go through some of the stages but not all of them. It all depends on our life history and on the losses, we have suffered in the past. Every loss in our life will rekindle our other past losses so much so that we will not only grieve for our present loss but also for all the losses that came before. In this respect it is important to mention that if in our first years of life our relationship with our caregivers was emotionally fragile, every loss that we will suffer later in life will be much more difficult to accept.

The process of grieving can be healthy or complicated. The symptoms of the latter are prolonged depression, i.e. lack of motivation to perform our daily tasks, anhedonia or inability to enjoy pleasurable activities, and often the wish to die to be reunited with the beloved. I remember one patient who was very attached to her father. The father suffered from heart problems and when he died and was being buried my patient felt a strong desire to jump into the grave. Although she resisted the impulse the intense feeling of loss stayed with her for many years until she was able to accept the death of her father as part of her life history.

However, loss is not all negative. As Eckart Tolle points out, loss and pain are our windows to a deeper reality where we will feel connected to all other human beings. Suffering is our road to becoming more compassionate beings. I once read that happy people don't have a history. It is true. It is only through pain that our life becomes wisdom.

"The natural way of being after the death of a loved one is suffering at first, then there is a deepening. In that deepening, you go to a place where there is no death." (*E. Tolle, video on loss.*) What Tolle means is that only the death of a loved one can give us the opportunity to reach that place where all is acceptance and finally peace. If we fall prey to depression, we will have a difficult time accepting reality and that peaceful place where all is acceptance will not be reached. On the contrary, when we are able to accept what is we will reach that place in ourselves that goes beyond the reality we see towards a more transcendent place.

Life is a journey where challenges and hurdles need to be faced in order for us to go forward and become the human beings we need to become. Loss is one of those challenges and it presents us with the very difficult task of having to accept it and move on. Like those heroes who have to undertake a long journey and solve many mysteries to become kings, we too have to learn how to face our losses one at a time.

----------O----------

The facilitator will distribute copies of Activity 3.

SESSION 4

SHOCK AND DISORGANIZATION

To live is to suffer.

To survive is to find some meaning in the suffering.

Friederich Nietzsche

The first stage after a significant loss will be the disorganization of our way of life. The routines we had established, the social network we used to rely on, our meals, our daily activities all of it will be looked upon under a different lens. In such a stage of disorganization most of us feel pervaded by a sense of futility and lack of purpose. At this stage the following symptoms can appear:

1. Hallucinations of the bereaved. These hallucinations are radically different from the hallucinations present in a psychosis due to the fact that they do not originate in the unconscious but on our conscious wish to see our loved one again.
2. Weight loss
3. Insomnia
4. Lack of energy
5. Anhedonia (inability to enjoy activities we previously enjoyed)
6. A sense of the vulnerability of life
7. Isolation
8. A feeling of void

In many ways the symptoms of the bereavement disorganization stage are similar to those of a clinical depression, especially the vegetative signs that have to do with weight and sleep. However, both are very different. In the case of bereavement, we can always remember the good moments spent with the deceased and those memories will provide us with a much-needed respite from our pain. On the other hand, when we are depressed nothing eases our feeling of emptiness. As Freud wrote in *Mourning and Melancholia*, **"during a depressive episode we turn our anger against ourselves rather than integrating our departed loved ones into our life."**

This statement by Freud that loved ones need to be integrated into our life seems to be totally opposite to Lindemann's theory that the bereaved should emancipate him or herself from the departed and generate new affective relationships. In fact, in 1996 a new book on grief called *Continuing Bonds: New Understanding of Grief (Klass, Silverman and Nickman)* offered a more realistic mourning paradigm. According to these authors **grief work does not imply emancipation from the deceased and the creation of new relations but on the contrary a new relationship should be established with the departed.**

During the stage of disorganization that follows the death of a loved one I believe it is wise to get busy putting things in order so as not to obsess with the loss we just suffered. As I mentioned in Session 1, having to prepare for the funeral and having to deal with family and friends will cloud reality for a while. Later, we could make use of the same process to live the first months after the death in a more absent state of mind. In a way, what I am proposing is to behave as if we did have the energy to do things until we are able to feel the energy again. Although often it is very difficult to pull ourselves together after suffering a significant loss, there is a way to trick our mind into helping us overcome the lack of energy that loss brings about. To accomplish this task, we need to follow 6 steps:

1. *Set a goal. For example: "I will start a new photo album with the pictures of my beloved and under each picture I will describe the moment it was taken."*
2. *Set a time to go buy the album.*
3. *Choose an album that has room for comments under each picture.*
4. *Make a design of the project*
5. *Gather all the pictures you can find*
6. *Start working on the project*

Working on a project related to the departed will allow us to channel our sadness into something creative, and the action of producing something will start removing the negativity of the loss from our mind.

Other examples
1. *Pick up a hobby that was favored by your departed*
2. *Gather letters, emails and other mementoes and make a book for you and your family. Give it out at Christmas or Rosh Hashanah to all those who will enjoy having it.*
3. *Plan a trip to the departed place of birth.*

4. *Write letters to his/her relatives to ask details about the departed's life that you never knew about.*

Almost all losses will bring about a reshuffling of roles: unless financially very comfortable, a widow will have to become the breadwinner, and often a widower will have to take care of children or household chores. In a more tragic situation, a parent will need to become either a childless parent or a parent with one less child. As we have already mentioned human beings have a very difficult time facing change, especially the change brought about by bereavement. In all areas of life, we are attracted by what is familiar and what is unknown is very difficult to assimilate. By and general what is unknown generates anxiety and fear.

Unfortunately, our only option is to gradually accept what has taken place in our lives and find a way to adapt to our new reality. Remember that in order to resolve our grief we will need to incorporate the loss into our life experience in a way that it will always be a reminder of those who were our companions in this journey. Eastern religions have pointed out that our significant others will still be with us in our next journey. If there are some unfinished business with our departed, and if we believe this to be true, we will have the opportunity in our next life to address those issues in a different way.

One of my patients told me once of a man she had met before she got married and who –this she understood after many years of marriage—would have been a much better partner than her now ex-husband. The man died in a crash when he was 60 years old. After her divorce my patient had several vivid dreams in which this man became very close to her. She is now convinced that she will meet him again after this life ends.

It goes without saying that these are very personal beliefs that not all of us share. As I mentioned before, grief is a very individual path and each one of us will travel a different road towards adjustment. I for one believe that human beings are made of energy and as such they don't disappear; they suffer a transformation. What this means is that those tendencies of ours that still need to be perfected will come back to life until we become what we are meant to become. Consequently, in our next journey some of our relationships from this life will be our companions again.

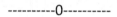

The facilitator will distribute copies of Activity 4.

SESSION 5

THE SERENITY PRAYER

God grant me the serenity
to accept the things, I cannot change;
the courage to change the things I can;
and the wisdom to know the difference.

As I already mentioned, in order to accept our losses, we need time; the more significant the loss the more time we will need to add it to our existential experience. Remember that a loss will never be overcome; hopefully we will adjust to a life without our beloved. In the best of circumstances, the losses we have suffered in the past have made us wiser and as time goes by, we have become more resilient to the challenges that come our way.

One issue that will deeply affect the way we grieve has to do with the kind of relationship we had with the departed. If the relationship was harmonious, the mourning process will be much more peaceful than if the relationship was plagued by misunderstandings. Furthermore, a dysfunctional relationship that left us with unfinished businesses will complicate the bereavement process to the point that it will probably become a prolonged depression, at least for a while. It is a well-known fact that a pathological mourning process can induce the bereaved to abuse alcohol and drugs or medication.

Loss can also affect our physical health. The relationship between body and mind is already a well-documented fact. The correlation between stress and physical wellbeing has been extensively researched. *"Several factors are related to the development of illness. Among the factors related to the development of illness are stress, coping style, and social support"* **(***D. Despues***, 1999.** *Stress and Illness.*) Several studies have shown a positive correlation between some illnesses and depression (i.e. hypertension, diabetes, coronary artery disease and stroke – *Paul J. Perry, Ph. D,* 2005.) I once met a father who lost his son to suicide. The son was a teenager and had always had with his father a very conflictive relationship. Sometime after his death the father fell sick and died of heart problems. He literally died of a broken heart.

Loss is undoubtedly our biggest life challenge. Unfortunately, like Judith Viorst stated in her wonderful book *Necessary Losses*, loss is unavoidable. Although human beings seem to be ill equipped to adapt to loss and change, there is no escape from this truth. Life is none other than impermanence. When we lose someone or something that we deem valuable our whole emotional and physical environment changes and a very arduous task suddenly makes its appearance: our need to adjust to a life that has lost one of its more significant components.

Already the pre-Socratic Greek philosopher Heraclitus alerted us in the V century BC that **"*no man ever steps in the same river twice*"**, a statement that reminds us of the impermanence of all things. At the same time the Buddha said to all those who were willing to listen that no human being can control the process of growing old, of falling sick and of passing away. The only option left to us is to accept our human condition and understand that the only way to enjoy life is to stay in the present moment. The more apt we are in adjusting to the present moment the more synchronicity we will feel with the whole Universe.

Accepting what cannot be changed is not an easy task. It can only be accomplished with time and after having reflected on the meaning of what happened to us. Those of us with a transcendent view of reality will sooner or later find a way to integrate their loss into the evolution of their lives. Those of us who do not believe in a life after death will have a harder time accepting a loss that is forever. Friederich Nietzsche said that what does not kill us makes us stronger. The reality is that losses don't make us stronger, they make us different. By losing what we love we change, becoming perhaps more introverted and more apt to reflect on life mysteries. We also feel the need for isolation and silence.

If each one of our losses was a thread of a different color and would be placed where it belonged in the tapestry of our life, the resulting pattern would show coherence and meaning. Without the integration of our losses our life pattern would be incomplete. Once losses are incorporated and understood then our whole existence will make sense and our anguish will gradually disappear. In other words, once we accept the fact that the person who died has completed his/her life cycle but will always be with us, our sadness will make room for a more peaceful view of life. But it's only at the end of our life that we will have a complete view of the meaning of our journey on earth. For the time being we can only speculate.

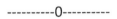

The facilitator will distribute copies of Activity 5.

SESSION 6

YOU WILL NEED TO FIND A SAFE PLACE WITHIN YOURSELF

When a storm approaches and somebody advices us to stay safe, we all understand what it means: that we need to find shelter. However, when several years ago I went to see a psychotherapist after suffering an emotional loss and she suggested that I now needed to find a place where I felt safe, I could not grab the meaning of her words immediately. I was too confused. It was only many years later that I understood that in order to face our life challenges we all need a place where we can withdraw and feel safe.

When we are in pain and life is just a heavy burden, our first impulse is to reach out and ask others for support. This reaching out is very appropriate and beneficial during the first months after having suffered a loss. However, it will come a time when we will feel that no matter how many friends we encounter or how much support they provide to us, the void that has pervaded our life after the loss is still there alive and well. It is then that we understand that our whole existence needs to be examined in a way that can only be done in solitude.

Some years after my loss I started feeling the need to be alone. It was then that I remembered my therapist's words so I started trying to figure out how I could find that safe place she had mentioned. Not an easy task for sure because this is language that cannot be explained, it can only be understood through intuition. I will try to describe the way I dealt with this task so that my readers can follow it if they need to do so.

The first thing I realized was that after a while of being with friends I suddenly felt this urge to go home and think. The stimulus that others provided me became too much to bear and a sort of weariness got hold of me. At those moments I went home and, after going to bed, I could sense in the silence of my bedroom a different kind of reality filling the void I usually felt inside me. It was an unknown realm where I did not feel alone anymore. It was a dreamlike space conducive to thought and reflection. Those were moments of deep immersion into the ups and downs of my existence, as well as the relationships that had come in and out of my life. The silence and the darkness provided me with much needed rest and tranquility, and it was then that I understood the meaning of the word safe. I realized that I was lucky enough to have a space in my life where nobody could interfere with my longing and my memories. But most important, while I was lying there in this safe physical place, I was able to access the most important safe place of all: the one within myself. When I am in that place, I know that everything evolves in the best possible way.

Accessing a safe place within ourselves is a humbling task that involves much thought. Many people I know will access this part of themselves through meditation, jogging, praying, or walking. I access it through thought. After a negative experience takes place in my life and after the pain or the anger have subsided, I go inside myself. I do this by reviewing what has happened to try to understand my role in the event. In the case of a loss by death there is really nothing to understand and the only thing I can do is accept this fact: that things happen in our life that we cannot explain. Our only option is to trust our journey. Deep down I know that at the end of the day these losses had to happen, and that the Universe does not make mistakes. It is this trust that enables me to access a deep part of myself where I always feel that I am on the right path.

Since a safe place within needs a physical setting, this setting needs to be inviting. If it is our bedroom, photographs of friends and family, especially of the departed, will provide the room with a sense of the continuity of life after death. A plant or some flowers will also add to the sacredness of the room, as well as incense or other aromatic sticks. The most important thing however is that we make sure that while in retreat we are allowed privacy for at least a couple of hours, especially in the first months of bereavement. Silence and solitude are the only way to access our inner self.

I mentioned at the beginning of this book that in order to mourn a loss we need to find a meaning to what has happened in our lives. I also added that the goal was not to justify the death of a loved one but to try to discover what this death and this suffering have brought to us in terms of wisdom. As I see it, as we work through our suffering, we will unearth many truths about ourselves, about the relationship that has just ended, about our conflicts and our moments of happiness that will need to be added to the tapestry of our entire existence. It is not for us to understand the death of a fellow human being. They are the only ones who know why their time has come. If we trust the Universe, we accept that a death never happens by mistake, but its cause is only known by the person who passed. The bereaved can only mourn and trust that the laws of the universe work in perfect synchronicity, and that when our time comes each one of us will know why our life has come to an end.

----------0----------

The facilitator will distribute copies of Activity 6.

SESSION 7

THE PROCESS OF GRIEVING

As we have seen throughout the pages of this book, bereavement is a process that has to be lived through and that cannot be avoided. If we resist facing our grief it will catch up with us at a later date, perhaps as a severe clinical depression. So, after the first weeks or months following the death of a loved one the time will come for us to start mourning and incorporating the loss into our life. Grieving can be done:

1. In solitude.
2. With the help of a therapist.
3. In a support group.

Let's review the most important points highlighted throughout these pages:

1. A loss will never be overcome but we will learn to live without the person we lost.
2. Bereavement is an individual process. There are no set rules about how and

   when to start or end our mourning process.
3. Bereavement is not about forgetting the person who died; on the contrary, bereavement is about remembering this person and making him/her a significant part of our life.
4. Looking for a meaning to our loss does not mean justifying the death of a loved one but understanding

what that loss has taught us in terms of compassion, empathy and humility.

5. For those of us who believe that life does not end with death, the departed does not vanish but suffers a transformation and will be with us again.

There is still one very important point to consider when talking about the death of a loved one, and that is that with every death we will feel closer to our own demise. While our parents are alive, we still have the older generation acting as a shield between us and death. However, when the generation that comes before us dies, we are next in line.

Feeling closer to our own death will be a significant factor in our bereavement process since we will not only grieve for the person who passed but also for our own passing. With every death we die a little and every death will be a step forward and towards the end of our own life. As years go by, we will gradually start distancing ourselves from everyday concerns to start thinking about how we would like to face our demise. For Buddhists death is the entrance to a new life and as such we should try to die in peace and serenity. A death that takes place amidst confusion and fear is not a good way to start a new existence. That is why it is so important to live a life based on compassion, honesty, generosity and responsibility. Living to the best of our abilities is conducive to dying well. Let me finish by saying that death –other people's death and ours- is our most significant teacher. It is the awareness of death that induces us to develop our human potentiality in order to act impeccably. Such is the meaning of death.

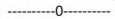

----------0----------

The facilitator will distribute copies of Activity 7.

SESSION 8

This session should be used by each participant to describe how the group was beneficial to him/her and what was its most important component. Each participant should start with the sentence:

What I am taking with me from this group is ... (expand.)

Participants can end their presentation by thanking other members for their help.

Alternatively, members can choose from the expressions in bold letters in the text and provide their own interpretation as to their meaning.

----------0----------

GROUP RULES

1. Maintain confidentiality. Group members and leader will keep private everything discussed in group.

2. Listen to others without interrupting. Wait for your turn to speak.

3. Respect other group members even if you don't agree with their opinion.

4. You won't be asked to participate if you don't feel comfortable. However, your participation is valuable for the group because we all learn from each other.

5. Turn off cellular phones

6. Comply with attendance. Every group member is an important part of the whole. When a member is not present the group will feel its absence.

ACTIVITIES

ACTIVITY 1

Please complete this activity in 10'.

1. *What do I expect to achieve by coming to group?*

ACTIVITY 1a

From the below words pick one that best describes what you are feeling at this stage of your mourning process.

SADNESS

LONELINESS

FEAR

ANGER

CONFUSION

UNABLE TO EXPRESS MY FEELINGS

FEELING DIFFERENT TO EVERYBODY ELSE

UNABLE TO FIND A PLACE WHERE TO FEEL SAFE

THE FEELING OF UNFINISHED BUSINESS WITH THE DEPARTED

THE FEELING THAT I WILL NEVER OVERCOME THE LOSS

THE WISH TO DIE

Note to facilitator: If any of the group members selects the last option, he/she should be directed to the nearest facility for treatment.

ACTIVITY 2

If I decide to resort to antidepressants, where can I find the name and number of a psychiatrist?

Where can I find support groups in the community?

Besides medication and support groups, what other resources can I tap into that would help my mourning process?

ACTIVITY 3

Think of a situation in the past that you needed to adjust to.

How did you do it?

How were you different after adjusting to what had happened?

ACTIVITY 4

What can my friends do for me that would make me feel better? ¿How can I ask them to do it?

¿What solitary activity can I perform that will make me feel better?

ACTIVITY 5

When I think of a past loss:

1. *How did it change me?*

   My daily life:

   My social life:

   My finances:

   My view of the world:

2. *Was I able to find a meaning to that loss?*

   Note: Finding a meaning to a loss does not mean that we are trying to justify the death of a loved one or explain a loss.

   Existential meanings can be the following:

   1. *Becoming more compassionate towards others*

   2. *Becoming more humble*

   3. *Wanting to help others in a situation of loss. Starting a group.*

4. *Starting a foundation*

5. *Becoming a speaker*

6. *Grasping the concept of the impermanence of all things*

ACTIVITY 6

RITUALS

Rituals have existed since the dawn of time and their goal is to highlight a significant change in our life. While the marriage ritual celebrates the end of our life as single people, funerals emphasize the end of our life in this world. The goal of rituals is to emphasize the transition.

Prepare a space in your home to use as a private space. If your home is small and there is no room, choose a spot in the yard or in a public park. Some people like to sit in the cemetery to feel closer to the departed. You should always use the same spot so as to become familiar with all its details: walls and photographs, or plants, flowers and animals. Sit in silence for the time of your choice, close your eyes, and focus on the memory of the deceased. When you feel him/her close to you, write his/her name on a piece of paper, his/her dates of birth and death, write the word Thank You and bury it in the earth or in a plant pot. Close your eyes again, breathe deeply and rest for a while. The acceptance of death will gradually sink into your unconscious mind.

What would you like to say to the deceased that you could not say when he/she was alive?

Thank your loved one for having been one of your life companions.

ACTIVITY 7

Write in a few words how you would like to be remembered after you pass away.

What should be the inscription on your tombstone?

With this activity we have reached the end of our journey together. I suggest that you keep all your writings in a safe place so that you can review them from time to time. As months and years go by perhaps you will feel the need to make changes to your notations. Remember that bereavement is a work in process and that it really never ends.

§

Printed in Great Britain
by Amazon

43059166R00030